Ya Sankofa!

A Book of Poetry

by

Torrance R. Harvey M.S. Ed.

DORRANCE
PUBLISHING CO
EST. 1920
PITTSBURGH, PENNSYLVANIA 15238

Dorrance Publishing Co
585 Alpha Drive
Suite 103
Pittsburgh, PA 15238
Visit our website at *www.dorrancebookstore.com*

ISBN: 978-1-4809-4279-0
eISBN: 978-1-4809-4302-5

Ya Sankofa!

Indigo

Inspired by the Rachel Weidkam (Painting of Lenny Kravitz)

When I face them Indigo blue skies
I look toward that light,
My shining star, she's so dainty.
Providing a reflection of who WE really are.
We are effervescent beings from other beings simply being
Shining stars, complex, simplistic, transparent, illusive
Traveling through space within our humanistic racecars, near and far.
Zoom Z-zoom...my music is pervasive
Boom B-boom...my music is pervasive
Our music is our alchemy...
So use your elements to create and go gold....
My music speaks volumes
It speaks volumes to many humanistic cars near and far...
So speak....
So speak, I say....SPEAK!
So if I speak about that spot where truth lies, I would sing those
memories of my
Children's future, so I could live a brighter now...
Now IS the essence of my domain, which contains all that was and will be...
Who will be singing YOUR next song and telling the correct human history?
My music speaks to my indigo blues stolen from Haiti
Like French colonial powers' inability to be creative,
Coffee beans and Cocoa
She's so dainty,
That's MY shining star...
She so dainty thus far... INDIGO

My Culture

(Circa Sept. 2013)

My culture stems from the beginning of time in human history, so pour the libation into the Atlantic and praise God for the birth and fossil resurrection of Lucy....

The oldest human fossil was found in Olduvai Gorge, Mother Africa...

So shout out the archaeological digs of Mary and Louis B. Leaky....and the significant sounds of natural resources being extracted from that land for consumption and obstructions, capitalist worldwide and to all to hell I send thee....

And finally my culture encompasses a bloody untold history that too captures the hidden colors of forever and colors of colorful rainbows....

As the thirteen moons divide themselves in cycles of twenty-three. Holy Father, Holy grail, sing praises for the Holy Trinity...

Study up, black boy, and learn the journey of human history...

Ghana, Songhai, and kingdoms of Mali...

Wrap this knowledge around your consciousness and dig the skin you're in...

How you count your days in time will confine, define, and hide the mind from greatness...so it's time to watch your sun rise and shine.

My culture stems from the beginning of...(pause)...time!

I am Man

When you see me...understand that there are layers within me that make me actually ME.

I AM MAN

I am a HUMAN.
A man of noble deeds!
I'm NOT a threat to your society.
You may say there are shades of gray
I say there are many shades of BLACK.
Black people have NEVER been a monolithic people
I am the man who raised pyramids when dawns were young and laid my burdens along the Congo when it lulled me to sleep...after your deep transgressions on Mother Africa.
So take time to comprehend the black man's complexities throughout human history.
Can you hear the mother drums hum the sounds of equality?
The eugenics movement in Germany contributed to this great divide in humanity.
Never question who I be...God knows.
He lets me call him me....
I am simply human....
I AM MAN.
I am a Black Man.

Inspiration

(Aug. 22, 2012)
Inspired by the events of the Martin Luther King Jr. Monument
The National Mall, Washington, D.C.

Oh, I've been inspired

By the bondage of ancestral roots that brought

hardworking payless people into the diaspora barefoot with NO boots....
I've been inspired.

I've been inspired by a people that took classical music and its modulations and converted the rhythmic drums of heavy BASS from a djembe BUM and turned its dissonant cords into greasy, nasty, MELLO cool thump, for elegant moments of soft moonlight and rhythmic FUNK...

Oh, I've been inspired.

I've been inspired by the mothers of the earth that belabored for nine months and provided an ETERNAL love to the universal existence of humanity in its truest sense...oh, I've been inspired...

I've been inspired by the mighty voices of JUSTICE when INJUSTICE somewhere posed a great threat to JUSTICE EVERYWHERE if you were of a particular hue....

So it's hard to force the YOUNG minds to believe and understand that it was those greats in human history to stage a revolutionary COUP 'd' etat....

Oh, I've been inspired...

I've been inspired by the sweltering heat of poverty within our inner cities that binds our youth into their gang activities filled with violence and existing as today's KRISTALLNACT deep within our city blocks, that also birthed a NEW genre of hip-hop called...hip-hop...which was supposed to be a FADE

so I was glad to hear Grandmaster Flash and Melly Mel shout out...

It's a jungle sometimes that make me wonder how I keep from going under...but let the family bring that light that penetrates the darkness...because light ONLY penetrates the darkness already there...and if we are gonna INSPIRE, that means to confront OUR great fears....

Fears of the unknown, to soar higher and higher, and again, I've been inspired...

Inspired by hand-to-hand feelings from an African-American President who once said, "...YES, I CAN!"

Inspiration. Peace!

Maybe

(Inspired by Will Smith and Jada Pinkett-Smith)

Maybe there are aspirations, hopes, and dreams I wanna pursue...

Maybe I was born to witness to God silently, with which the wind-blown spirits already knew

through my actions profound as the percussive sounds of boom-boom, just maybe thru and thru...

Maybe the Charles Street Projects in Poughkeepsie where I grew up within...is a powerful testimony, too!

Maybe, just maybe...

Well, maybe it's imperative that I connect with the rebirth of humanity in its truest sense...

and in the renaissance like in Harlem, simply me and you....

Maybe we are meant to be alone...alone to atone...

Because fear of the darkness is fear of the unknown.

Now look toward YOUR light because light only penetrates the darkness that's already there...this maybe thang....opens up an entire world of possibilities, and maybe this is the life that supersedes life's time I am

Think maybe!

Maya

(A Special Dedication to Maya Angelou), June 2014

She spoke to me in my sleep, telling me to go ahead and take a leap of faith to achieve my dreams that seem to escape me in my awakened state....

She spoke to me in my sleep as I ran through the fields of Mississippi filled with yellow daffodils that seemed endlessly filled with my thrills of a joyful occasion....

It was still early in the morning because I could feel the heat from an early-morning sunrise and its misty dew deep within the grassy roots brushing up against my work-boots...and bumblebees and pretty bright butterflies that too enjoyed that sunrise....

When she spoke to me in my sleep, I could hear the deep, rich texture in her voice, asking me, "Who are WE to block the human creativity...with which to witness and inspire others?? Who are WE to turn down God's vessel to speak to someone's despair? Who are WE to ignore the calling? Who are we to silence the message that will set someone completely free??"

She spoke to me in my sleep, and her voice came as a quick spiritual surprise...but just like life...I rise

I rise...and even with your twisted lies...yet I still rise. Thank you, Mother Maya!

What a Glare

(January 1995)

The moon twinkles with a glare.

It shines in dark nights that represent life and it not being fair.

The moon sits still as motion surrounds, while the black man has a spirit in the mist that screams from injustices that appear to be nonexistent in sound.

Why does that moon twinkle with a glare as the black man lives a life full of great fear and despair he and only other black men can hear?

SHINE, MOON, SHINE!

Exist with a HOPEFUL stare instead of that empty glare!

Metaphors

(September 2012)

My rhythm flows like metaphoric waters,

between narrow streams

because I'm that literary SUPERMAN SUPERimposed in

YOUR cosmetic fantastic dreams,

and hip-hop's founding fathers birthed my creativity BACK in the 80s

when block parties were filled with partygoers and NOT gun toters

who call themselves THUGS from the "School of Hard Knocks"

Ya JUST teenagers....

looking for a way out of the concrete JUNGLE blocks

so give ME a real taste of that purple haze I call purified real life

and find your way out of the dangerous JUNGLE MAZE

and don't believe that hype

and stop all that fightin'

Protect our inner-city youth

SHINE, MOON, SHINE!

Exist with a HOPEFUL stare instead of that empty glare!

Mr. Opportunity

Speak to me, Mr. Opportunity.

The Lady sings the blues and my hopes the wind done scattered, too....

And despair runs through my body like SHAZZAM!

But I know who the fuck I am...

And they say New York City...

But New York City, I put mad performance time in New York City streets...

Down them mean streets like Pari Thomas's philosophical descriptions and hypothetical

speech...Rough and tough blocks

And Central Park's beautiful tapestry...

Fast cars and hustle, too...

So send me a message and a signal, too!

I've got five mouths to feed

And trying to make ends meet, Mr. Opportunity.

Send me Mrs. Mercy....

Because Grace and Mercy were supposed to follow me all the days of my life.

Mr. Opportunity, where you be?

Well, I can't hear you!

Wait

Please....

Don't shoot...pow...pow....

Human Instruments in Poverty

(March 2013)

I tested my creativity when I was broke....

Like broken humdrums that hum in dark, silent nights

Looking for steady income to feed my family....

So how does the government benefit me....individually and

collectively as I exist somewhere in between skit and skat and that of

rat like in an urban setting filled with violence and sociological paradigms that consume

the minds of yuppie students and college professors that profess about poverty in those

theoretical hypothetical sociological courses....

I'm sick of watching TV and wishing that the fictional characters were simply me.

So guess who's coming to dinner?

But there's no dinner to eat because of generational poverty, and guess who's up next?

I believe that's me....on this turn because every turn is my turn when you are alone

objectively stricken by poverty.

Passionate Love

She walked into my life
I just knew it was the windblown spirits that aligned the cosmic stars right...
She was my fantasy from way back in the days, ya see...
A beautiful human soliloquy, out of darkness, shining so brightly...
She became my motivation
I became her transportation to the North Side of education.
It was musical powers that played softly within the universal lessons
of rhythmic rhymes and reasons...that brought us together
The cosmic mix of human perfection
A mix of body chemistry, which is like an anomaly
So powerful and indescribable that we had to make love
all night under the prettiest moonlight of darkness...with the sounds of
the ocean
our love is like for real this time...but because of given circumstances
we became like two ships passing in the night
not knowing if we could ever encounter again that very special
light...called love.

Happy Valentine's

(February 2000)

True to you

And ah

True to me...

Love can be a spectacle

for one to see....

Life's got all kinds of

Twists and turns that

Make our love go 'round and 'round;

You're the BEST lowdown Valentine in EVERY

Town....

So continue to SHINE

Happy Valentine's, "Duke"....

Music

(April 2012)

If I were to travel the innermost thoughts of the universal emotions of man, I'd capture the transcendental vibrations of emotional sound piercing the dissonant melodies of subtext...bequeath in hot seats...of lava beneath hollow grounds.

My quiet spirit would fly high beyond the green trees and green pastures of imagination and improvisation, skit-scatting like colorful jazz played by street musicians, keeping the rhythmic timing by tapping his feet in broken shoes filled with tattered sores of his feet.

So I can see your color, I can see the color of life free from strife and anger that will set me free, connecting me to my own eternal love, incubated and immersed within the yolk of maternal splendor...

A cool splendor filled with calm, refreshing revelations of timbre within rhythmic syncopations of groove on a vintage vibe.

Vibe must be vibe...so check the rhyme, yo, check the rhyme.

Iambic pentameter beats and measures filled with the correct rhythmic timing 'cause timing is everything.

Especially if I were to travel the innermost thoughts of the universal emotions of man...

I'd capture the dimensions of human performance with one note.

MUSIC!

The Lion and the King

Sometimes I must move slowly like a cat...
Sometimes I must move with dispatch.
There are times I must be silent, unheard.
Just like the morning spring sun shining over the harmonious tweeting birds.
Then, there is that one moment in time I must ROAR loudly
For everyone to hear and fear everywhere.
Bringing their hearts and minds to understand ONE THING.
I AM the TRUE Lion and the King!

Alive

(June 2012)

When I saw the break of day
I could silently say, the sun shined brightly upon me...
day after day, even when I was a child,
Momma taught me real unconditional love, unspeakable in words, you see.
It's a feeling that would make me run...to her...catching teardrops
in my hand every time I think about her spirit, which lifts me high...
SO I wish I could fly,
hence I must BE fly
simply because I am ALIVE.
Alive, Alive, ALIVE!
Life is a splendid journey....

Joy

(A Special Poem for Luciana)
(A Child Cancer Patient)
(April 9, 2014)

Open your eyes so you can see what I see...clear blue skies...with the cosmic energy of a sunrise...that abides in the human spirit of coy...

Yet awakened by the scent of nature's beauty of life and joy...joy that comes out of the playful human hut of history...so that we can share with music and dance collectively.

So we must celebrate the gold mines of life, Luciana...capturing happy moments like hum-drums that hum in dark, silent nights. Be proud of the mothers that bring forth the light in our children of the night...who care and share like rippling echoes of

eternity...rising like the high tides in oceans of divinity....

Open your eyes so you can see the beauty that I can see...can you hear the wind blowing through the trees...of eternity? She's our shining star...she's so dainty thus far...and forever, never, ever... far....

Solar Energy

By Armani Harvey and Torrance Harvey

Home solar energy is on the rise,

Its energy source has an unlimited supply.

The rise of the solar cells comes from the sun.

Like energy from generators transferring solar cells...illuminating light
very bright for vision in darkness to bring forth the light...to give all in
the house vision and sight.

The Solar One power station uses heat to make steam that penetrates
and permeates throughout the room during cold, cold winter nights.

Humans have done wonderful things in solar science...

right?

Prayer

(October 29, 2012)

Dear Lord:

I'm not gonna front...I'm a little nervous about this storm hitting us tonight as predicted...BUT I know a God who's known as an ALL-Mighty God who sits up high and looks down low...a God who gave us his only begotten son, Jesus, ya know...who provides me a CALM during a time of storms....

'Cause I already got storms in my life brewing before Sandy...so I say this all to say...I am in deep prayer...meditation coupled with a whole lot of conviction right now...and I pray to you one more time for all of our family's safety and ability to weather THIS storm tumbling down and all other storms present in our lives right now....

Permeate your protective hands upon us so no hurt, harm, or danger can overtake us in our given circumstance.... Your care can't weaken the will of the poor, for the meek shall inherit the earth...and I know that the greatest weakness of man is not believing...but I do believe in you....

In Jesus' Name...Gods' people say...AMEN!

The Hurricane Came from Sandy

(October 29, 2012)

Writing poetry...as the hurricane approaches...to create metaphoric literary form to blow minds like acrobatic syncopated brainstorms...like freedom fest...writing and creating pathways of intellectual syncopated sound waves that stimulate your cerebral cortex...releasing that real-life pain...so go tell this on the mountain to Sandy and care less about the rain...let it rain, let it rain....

Go tell Saul Williams that Harvey feels his pain...when he spoke about not being the son of Cha Clack Clack...because we are before

that free your minds and elect the President

whose deeds will INDEED supersede life's time...with a steady hand to guide us through the most difficult economic times of this era and time...so it is almost THAT time to reflect...select...and check

yourself before you wreck yourself in this here life...and...

if I were to travel the innermost thoughts of the universal emotions of man...I'd capture the transcendental vibrations of emotional sounds piercing the dissonant melodies of subtext...

skit-scatting like colorful jazz played by street musicians in the hurricane...keeping the rhythmic timing by tapping his feet in broken shoes filled with tattered sores on his feet...don't stop the rain...can you stand the rain, Boyz to Men...

so listen to the storm's music...and hear the music of...nature!

Real, Real Love

True to you and, ah...true to me

Love can be a spectacle for one to really see.

It could be sweet like nectar stock

Fingertips massaging that sweet spot

Observing the heat of passionate love like hot, hot, hot.

It could be the best lowdown love around town.

Never sour...

Never rotten...

FRESH!

So I keep my eyes on the sun, while you digest the moonlight....

Love's light when it's right.

Not forced upon me

Cannot refuse it...

Must give account if I misuse it or abuse it.

So let's keep love real tight.

Right?

It's that real, real love, and I say it's all right....